WHSmith

CW01652343

Quick Revision

KS2: Age 7–8

Spelling

Louis Fidge

First published 2007
exclusively for WHSmith by
Hodder Education, an Hachette UK Company, 338 Euston Road, London NW1 3BH

Impression number 10 9 8 7 6 5 4 3
Year 2010

A CIP record for this book is available from the British Library.

Cover illustration: Sally Newton Illustrations

Typeset by Fakenham Photosetting Limited, Fakenham, Norfolk

ISBN 978 0 340 94987 0

Printed and bound in the UK by Hobbs the Printers.

For parents

Quick Revision: Spelling

- Spelling is a key feature of the National Curriculum and the National Literacy Framework.
- Children need to be able to spell in order to read and write fluently and confidently.
- Good spelling is essential in all areas of the curriculum.
- Learning to spell requires constant practice and reinforcement.
- This series of 'teach and test' books will help build your child's confidence and ability in spelling.

Features of the books

- Each unit:
  - has a clear spelling focus
  - introduces ten words which contain the same spelling focus
  - has a range of activities which help your child to learn to spell the words
  - finishes with a spelling test, using the ten Test words.
- Answers to the activities may be found on pages 24–27.
- A record sheet is provided on page 3 on which your child can keep a record of all test scores.

How to do the units

- Do one spelling unit and test each week.
- Agree on a set time with your child, and keep it the same each week if possible.
- Ensure your child can read the Test words at the top of the page and knows their meanings.
- Encourage your child to do the activities to help learn the words.
- On completion of the activities, get your child to do the unit test.

How to do the spelling tests

- Turn to pages 28–32 and find the appropriate answer sheet to complete.
- Ask your child to look back at the Test words in the unit and study these again for a short while.
- Then either:
  - copy out the words and read them slowly to your child (or get another adult or child to read them)

  or:
  - ask your child to write the words from memory (without copying them!)
- When the spelling test has been completed, ask your child to mark it by referring back to the Test words and checking their spellings.
- Colour in the score out of ten.
- After each test, ask your child to fill in the results on the record sheet on page 3.

Spelling test record sheet

Score																				
10																				
9																				
8																				
7																				
6																				
5																				
4																				
3																				
2																				
1																				
	1	2	3	4	5	6	7	8	9	10	11	12	13	14	15	16	17	18	19	20

Test

Unit 1: **ear** and **eer**

Test words

d____	y____	h____	cl____	app____
d____	p____	ch____	st____	engin____

1. Add **ear** to the end of the top five words in the box above.
   Add **eer** to the end of the bottom five words in the box above.
   Read the ten Test words you make.

2. Write the **ear** words in alphabetical order.

   ________ ________ ________ ________ ________

3. Write the **eer** words in alphabetical order.

   ________ ________ ________ ________ ________

4. Choose the correct word for each sentence.
   a) A ________ (dear, deer) has four legs.
   b) The new car was very ________ (dear, deer).
   c) There are twelve months in a ________ (hear, year).
   d) On a ________ (peer, clear) night you can see lots of stars.
   e) An ________ (appear, engineer) mends engines.
   f) The crowd gave a loud ________ (cheer, steer).

5. Now do **Spelling Test 1** on page 28.

Unit 2: **or**

Test words

t___ch   sail___   h___n   doct___   f___t

act___   sp___t   visit___   st___m   auth___

1. Add the missing **or** to each word in the box above. Read the ten Test words you make.

2. Complete the chart.

words with **or** inside them	words with **or** at the end

3. Write the words with:

   a) four letters ______ ______

   b) five letters ______ ______ ______ ______

   c) six letters ______ ______ ______

   d) seven letters ______

4. Now do **Spelling Test 2** on page 28.

Unit 3: **ore** and **oor**

Test words

c____	m____	sn___	sc___	sh___
d___	p___	m___	fl___	ind___s

1. Add **ore** to the end of the top five words in the box above.
Add **oor** to the bottom five words in the box above.
Read the ten Test words you make.

2. Choose the correct word for each sentence.
a) I want some _________ (moor, more) cake, please.
b) I went for a walk on the _________ (moor, more).

3. Which **ore** word:
a) do you do in your sleep? ____________
b) is in an apple? ____________
c) is by the seaside? ____________
d) do you do in football? ____________

4. Which **oor** word:
a) is the opposite of rich? ____________
b) is the opposite of outdoors? ____________
c) can you open? ____________
d) can you walk on? ____________

5. Now do **Spelling Test 3** on page 28.

Unit 4: **aw**

Test words

s___	j___	cl___	p___	dr___
l___n	y___n	cr___l	h___k	___ful

1. Add the missing **aw** to each word in the box above. Read the ten Test words you make.

2. Which words:

   a) begin with **aw**? ______

   b) end with **aw**? _____ _____ _____ _____ _____

   c) have **aw** in the middle? _____ _____ _____ _____

3. Underline the **aw** words in the sentences.

   a) The lion hurt a claw on one paw.

   b) I saw the boy draw an awful picture.

   c) I yawn when I am tired.

   d) My baby brother likes to crawl on the lawn.

   e) My jaw moves when I eat.

   f) The hawk flew high in the sky.

4. Now do **Spelling Test 4** on page 28.

Unit 5: au

Test words

h___l l___nch t___nt p___se s___ce
h___nt ___tumn s___cer l___ndry n___ghty

1. Add **au** to each word in the box above.
   Read the ten Test words you make.

2. Write the first five words in alphabetical order.

   ________ ________ ________ ________ ________

3. Write the second five words in alphabetical order.

   ________ ________ ________ ________ ________

4. Write the word that means:

   a) a season ________ **b)** what ghosts do ________
   c) to pull ________ **d)** to take off ________
   e) a cup goes on it ________
   f) to make fun of someone ________
   g) badly-behaved ________
   h) dirty washing ________
   i) you put it on food ________
   j) to stop for a while ________

5. Now do **Spelling Test 5** on page 29.

Unit 6: er

Test words

k___b	farm___	t___m	paint___	p___ch
climb___	sw___ve	sing___	st___n	build___

1 Add the missing **er** to each word in the box above. Read the ten Test words you make.

2 Complete the chart.

words with **er** inside them	words with **er** at the end

3 What do you call a person who:

a) paints? ____________ **b)** builds? ____________
c) climbs? ____________ **d)** farms? ____________
e) sings? ____________

4 Which word means:

a) part of a pavement? ____________
b) part of a school year? ____________
c) very serious? ____________
d) what a bird stands on? ____________
e) move suddenly to one side? ____________

5 Now do **Spelling Test 6** on page 29.

Unit 7: ir

Test words

b___d	g___l	sh___t	d___ty	f___st
th___st	th___d	th___ty	wh___l	sk___t

1. Add the missing **ir** to each word in the box above. Read the ten Test words you make.

2. Change some letters. Read the new words you make.

   a) Change the **b** in **b**ird to **th** *third*

   b) Change the **g** in **g**irl to **wh** ____________

   c) Change the **sh** in **sh**irt to **sk** ____________

   d) Change the **d** in **d**irty to **th** ____________

   e) Change the **f** in **f**irst to **th** ____________

   f) Change the **th** in **th**ird to **b** ____________

   g) Change the **wh** in **wh**irl to **g** ____________

   h) Change the **sk** in **sk**irt to **sh** ____________

   i) Change the **th** in **th**irty to **d** ____________

   j) Change the **th** in **th**irst to **f** ____________

3. Now do **Spelling Test 7** on page 29.

Unit 8: **ur**

Test words

b___n	t___f	n___se	c___t	t___n
p___se	c___l	h___t	h___l	s___f

1. Add the missing **ur** to each word in the box above. Read the ten Test words you make.

2. Write the word that rhymes with:

   a) burn ________ **b)** turf ________

   c) nurse ________ **d)** curt ________

   e) curl ________

3. Choose the correct word in each sentence.

   a) A fire will ______ (burn, turn).

   b) The foam made by waves at sea is called ______ (surf, turf).

   c) She put her money in her ________ (nurse, purse).

   d) I ______ (curt, hurt) myself when I fell off my bike.

   e) To ______ (curl, hurl) means to throw something.

4. Now do **Spelling Test 8** on page 29.

Unit 9: **ch** and **ph**

Test words

an___or s___ool ___oir e___o ___emist

ele___ant ___oto al___abet tele___one gra___

1. Add the missing **ch** to the top five words in the box above.
   Add the missing **ph** to the bottom five words.
   Read the ten Test words you make.

2. Choose **ch** or **ph** to complete each word.
   a) e___o **b)** ___oto **c)** al___abet **d)** ___oir
   e) ele___ant **f)** s___ool **g)** tele___one
   h) ___emist **i)** an___or **j)** gra___

3. Underline the Test words. Write the Test words here.
   a) q w r p h o t o p m x z *photo*
   b) a n c h o r b g d s v c ___________
   c) p l k h t z s c h o o l ___________
   d) k d f a l p h a b e t n ___________
   e) b e l e p h a n t x t ___________
   f) c h e m i s t c b m b s ___________
   g) k t r w s e c h o z w q ___________
   h) n c h o i r t r w x y u ___________
   i) k t e l e p h o n e g k ___________
   j) w q f s z d v g r a p h ___________

4. Now do **Spelling Test 9** on page 30.

Unit 10: Compound words

Test words

rainbow	butterfly	sunshine	toothbrush	handbag
windmill	moonlight	bookcase	playground	seaside

1. Read the ten Test words above.

2. Write the top five words in alphabetical order.

   ________ ________ ________ ________ ________

3. Write the bottom five words in alphabetical order.

   ________ ________ ________ ________ ________

4. Complete each word to make a Test word.

   a) wind______ **b)** sun_____ **c)** hand_____

   d) butter____ **e)** moon_____ **f)** _____bow

   g) _____case **h)** ____side **i)** ______ground

   j) _____brush

5. Now do **Spelling Test 10** on page 30.

Unit 11: Syllables

Test words

pencil	dentist	tractor	lemon	carpet
teacher	donkey	ankle	camel	garden

1. Read the ten Test words above. Each word contains two syllables.
   Tap out the syllables as you read each word: pen/cil.

2. Do these syllable sums.
   a) trac + tor = *tractor* **b)** lem + on = _______
   c) don + key = _______ **d)** an + kle = _______
   e) den + tist = _______ **f)** tea + cher = _______
   g) gar + den = _______ **h)** cam + el = _______
   i) pen + cil = _______ **j)** car + pet = _______

3. Write the second syllable of each word.
   a) trac____ **b)** an____ **c)** pen_____ **d)** cam____
   e) don____ **f)** tea____ **g)** den_____ **h)** gar___
   i) car____ **j)** lem____

4. Write the first syllable of each word.
   a) ____on **b)** ____den **c)** ____cil **d)** ____tor
   e) ____cher **f)** ____el **g)** ____key **h)** ____pet
   i) ____tist **j)** ____kle

5. Now do **Spelling Test 11** on page 30.

Unit 12: Double consonants

Test words

button	rabbit	apple	address	digger
pillow	tunnel	summer	hiccup	mirror

1. Read the ten Test words above. Each word contains a double consonant in the middle and is made of two syllables.
   Tap out the syllables as you read each word: but/ton.

2. Do these syllable sums.
   a) rab + bit = *rabbit* **b)** ad + dress = ______
   c) hic + cup = ______ **d)** sum + mer = ______
   e) ap + ple = ______ **f)** but + ton = ______
   g) pil + low = ______ **h)** tun + nel = ______
   i) mir + ror = ______ **j)** dig + ger = ______

3. Write the second syllable of each word.
   a) sum____ **b)** but____ **c)** ad_____ **d)** hic____
   e) tun____ **f)** rab____ **g)** mir_____ **h)** ap___
   i) dig____ **j)** pil____

4. Write the first syllable of each word.
   a) ____ror **b)** ____cup **c)** ____mer **d)** ____nel
   e) ____low **f)** ____ger **g)** ____dress **h)** ____ple
   i) ____bit **j)** ____ton

5. Now do **Spelling Test 12** on page 30.

Unit 13: -le

Test words

jung___	simp___	crumb___	sprink___	hand___
tang___	purp___	ramb___	spark___	need___

1. Add the missing **le** to the end of each word in the box above. Read the ten Test words you make.
2. Complete the chart.

-ble words	**-dle** words	**-gle** words	**-kle** words	**-ple** words

3. Choose the correct word for each sentence.

a) A lion lives in the __________ (jungle, tangle).
b) These spellings are very ________ (purple, simple)!
c) I like apple ___________ (crumble, ramble).
d) I _________ (sparkle, sprinkle) water on the earth.
e) The door __________ (handle, needle) is broken.
f) The string was in a terrible ______ (jungle, tangle).
g) __________ (Purple, Simple) is my favourite colour.
h) I ____________ (crumble, ramble) in the country.
i) Gold coins __________ (sparkle, sprinkle).
j) I pricked my finger with the ____ (handle, needle).

4. Now do **Spelling Test 13** on page 31.

Unit 14: Silent letters **k**, **w** and **g**

Test words

knee	**wrist**	**knife**	**write**	**gnome**
gnaw	**knock**	**wrap**	**know**	**wriggle**

1. Read the ten Test words.
(Note: The first letter in each word is **silent**, and is not pronounced.)

2. Which words begin with a silent:
a) **w**? ________ ________ ________ ________
b) **k**? ________ ________ ________ ________
c) **g**? ________ ________

3. Which word means:
a) to chew? ________
b) a part of your arm? ________
c) a part of your leg? ________
d) something you cut with? ________
e) to put paper around something? ________
f) to strike something hard? ________
g) to learn something and remember it? ________
h) to twist and turn? ________
i) to make marks on paper that someone can read? ________
j) a goblin? ________

4. Now do **Spelling Test 14** on page 31.

Unit 15: Silent letters **b** and **l**

Test words

comb	talk	lamb	calm	climb
calf	thumb	half	bomb	walk

1. Read the ten Test words.
(Note: The letter in **bold** in each word is **silent**, and is not pronounced.)

2. Which words have a silent:
a) **b**? ________ ________ ________ ________ ________
b) **l**? ________ ________ ________ ________ ________

3. Which word means:
a) a young sheep? ____________
b) part of your hand? ____________
c) something that explodes? ____________
d) a young cow? ____________
e) not rough? ____________
f) something you do to your hair? ____________
g) to speak? ____________
h) to go up? ____________
i) one of two equal pieces? ____________
j) to move along on foot? ____________

4. Now do **Spelling Test 15** on page 31.

Unit 16: The prefixes **un-** and **dis-**

Test words

___fair	___well	___lucky	___true	___kind
___agree	___trust	___obey	___appear	___honest

1. Add the prefix **un** to the top five words in the box above.
   Add the prefix **dis** to the bottom five words in the box above.
   Read the ten Test words you make.

2. Choose **un** or **dis** to begin each of these words.

   a) ___well **b)** ___appear **c)** ___trust **d)** ___lucky
   e) ___fair **f)** ___obey **g)** ___honest **h)** ___true
   i) ___kind **j)** ___agree

3. Which Test word means the opposite of:

   a) lucky? ___________ **b)** obey? ___________
   c) appear? ___________ **d)** agree? ___________
   e) true? ___________ **f)** kind? ___________
   g) trust? ___________ **h)** honest? ___________
   i) fair? ___________ **j)** well? ___________

4. Now do **Spelling Test 16** on page 31.

Unit 17: The suffixes -ful and -less

Test words

use____	colour____	power____	thought___	help___
use____	colour____	power____	thought___	help___

1. Add the suffix **ful** to the top five words.
   Add the suffix **less** to the bottom five words.
   Read the ten Test words you make.

2. Which Test word means the opposite of:
   a) useful? __________ **b)** helpful? __________
   c) powerful? __________ **d)** thoughtful? __________
   e) colourful? __________ **f)** powerless? __________
   g) helpless? __________ **h)** colourless? __________
   i) useless? __________ **j)** thoughtless? __________

3. Choose the correct word for each sentence.
   a) I do lots of jobs at home because I like to be __________ (helpful, helpless).
   b) The painting was bright and __________ (colourful, colourless).
   c) The TV is broken and __________ (useful, useless).
   d) The __________ (thoughtful, thoughtless) boy pushed the girl out of his way.
   e) The __________ (powerful, powerless) man picked up the heavy weight.

4. Now do **Spelling Test 17** on page 32.

Unit 18: The suffix -ing

Test words

biting	smiling	hiding	riding	driving
wagging	winning	shutting	digging	running

1. Read the ten Test words above. They are all **verbs**.
2. Complete the charts with the correct Test words.

verb	add **ing**
hide	*hiding*
drive	
bite	
ride	
smile	

verb	add **ing**
shut	
run	
win	
wag	
dig	

3. Write the correct form of the verb in each sentence.

a) The girl was ___________ (hide) behind the tree.
b) The boy was ___________ (run) very fast.
c) I like ___________ (win) races.
d) I am ___________ (ride) my new bike.
e) The girl is ___________ (smile) at her friend.
f) The pirate was ___________ (dig) up the treasure.
g) My dad likes ___________ (drive) the car.
h) The dog was ___________ (wag) its tail.
i) The child is ___________ (bite) an apple.
j) The lady was ___________ (shut) her bag.

4. Now do **Spelling Test 18** on page 32.

Unit 19: Key words (1)

Test words

angry frightened pleased miserable cross
unhappy shy bored excited lonely

1. Read the ten Test words. They are all to do with feelings.
2. Write the top five words in alphabetical order.

   ________ ________ ________ ________ ________
3. Write the bottom five words in alphabetical order.

   ________ ________ ________ ________ ________
4. Fill in the missing vowels. Then write the whole word again.

   a) m_i_s_e_r_a_bl_e_ *miserable*
   b) __xc__t__d ________
   c) fr__ght__n__d ________
   d) b__r__d ________
   e) pl__ __s__d ________
   f) cr__ss ________
   g) __ngr__* ________
   h) __nh__pp__* ________
   i) l__n__l__* ________
   j) sh__* ________

   * Note: In these words the **y** acts as a 'part-time' vowel.
5. Now do **Spelling Test 19** on page 32.

Unit 20: Key words (2)

Test words

bellowed joked grumbled exclaimed murmured whispered howled demanded pleaded shouted

1. Read the ten Test words. They are all 'dialogue' words that you can use instead of 'said' when you are writing.
2. Write the top five words in alphabetical order.

   ________ ________ ________ ________ ________

3. Write the bottom five words in alphabetical order.

   ________ ________ ________ ________ ________

4. Fill in the missing vowels. Then write the whole word again.

   a) j__k__d ____________
   b) d__m__nd__d ____________
   c) sh__ __t__d ____________
   d) b__ll__w__d ____________
   e) gr__mbl__d ____________
   f) pl__ __d__d ____________
   g) h__wl__d ____________
   h) wh__sp__r__d ____________
   i) __xcl__ __m__d ____________
   j) m__rm__r__d ____________

5. Now do **Spelling Test 20** on page 32.

Answers

Unit 1

1 dear year hear clear appear deer peer cheer steer engineer

2 appear clear dear hear year

3 cheer deer engineer peer steer

4 a deer b dear c year d clear e engineer f cheer

Unit 2

1 torch sailor horn doctor fort actor sport visitor storm author

2 words with **or** inside them: torch horn fort sport storm
words with **or** at the end: sailor doctor actor visitor author

3 a horn fort
b torch actor sport storm
c sailor doctor author
d visitor

Unit 3

1 core more snore score shore door poor moor floor indoors

2 a more b moor

3 a snore b core c shore d score

4 a poor b indoors c door d floor

Unit 4

1 saw jaw claw paw draw lawn yawn crawl hawk awful

2 a awful
b saw jaw claw paw draw
c lawn yawn crawl hawk

3 a The lion hurt a claw on one paw.
b I saw the boy draw an awful picture.
c I yawn when I am tired.
d My baby brother likes to crawl on the lawn.
e My jaw moves when I eat.
f The hawk flew high in the sky.

Unit 5

1 haul launch taunt pause sauce haunt autumn saucer laundry naughty

2 haul launch pause sauce taunt

3 autumn haunt laundry naughty saucer

4 a autumn b haunt c haul d launch e saucer f taunt g naughty h laundry i sauce j pause

Unit 6

1 kerb farmer term painter perch climber swerve singer stern builder

2 words with **er** inside them: kerb term perch swerve stern
words with **er** at the end: farmer painter climber singer builder

3 a painter b builder c climber d farmer e singer

4 a kerb b term c stern d perch e swerve

Unit 7

1 bird girl shirt dirty first thirst third thirty whirl skirt

2 a third b whirl c skirt d thirty e thirst f bird g girl h shirt i dirty j first

Unit 8

1 burn turf nurse curt turn purse curl hurt hurl surf

2 a turn b surf c purse d hurt e hurl

3 a burn b surf c purse d hurt e hurl

Unit 9

1 anchor school choir echo chemist elephant photo alphabet telephone graph

2 a echo b photo c alphabet d choir e elephant f school g telephone h chemist i anchor j graph

3 a q w r p h o t o p m x z photo
b a n c h o r b g d s v c anchor
c p l k h t z s c h o o l school
d k d f a l p h a b e t n alphabet
e n b e l e p h a n t x t elephant
f c h e m i s t c b m b s chemist
g k t r w s e c h o z w q echo
h n c h o i r t r w x y u choir
i k t e l e p h o n e g k telephone
j w q f s z d v g r a p h graph

Unit 10

2 butterfly handbag rainbow sunshine toothbrush

3 bookcase moonlight playground seaside windmill

4 a windmill b sunshine c handbag d butterfly e moonlight f rainbow g bookcase h seaside i playground j toothbrush

Unit 11

2 a tractor b lemon c donkey
d ankle e dentist f teacher
g garden h camel i pencil
j carpet

3 a tractor b ankle c pencil
d camel e donkey f teacher
g dentist h garden i carpet
j lemon

4 a lemon b garden c pencil
d tractor e teacher f camel
g donkey h carpet i dentist
j ankle

Unit 12

2 a rabbit b address
c hiccup d summer
e apple f button
g pillow h tunnel
i mirror j digger

3 a summer b button
c address d hiccup
e tunnel f rabbit
g mirror h apple
i digger j pillow

4 a mirror b hiccup
c summer d tunnel
e pillow f digger
g address h apple
i rabbit j button

Unit 13

1 jungle simple crumble
sprinkle handle tangle purple
ramble sparkle needle

2 **-ble** words: crumble ramble
-dle words: handle needle
-gle words: jungle tangle
-kle words: sprinkle sparkle
-ple words: simple purple

3 a jungle b simple c crumble
d sprinkle e handle f tangle
g Purple h ramble i sparkle
j needle

Unit 14

2 a wrist write wrap wriggle
b knee knife knock know
c gnome gnaw

3 a gnaw b wrist c knee
d knife e wrap f knock
g know h wriggle i write
j gnome

Unit 15

2 a comb lamb climb thumb bomb
b talk calm calf half walk

3 a lamb b thumb c bomb
d calf e calm f comb
g talk h climb i half
j walk

Unit 16

1 unfair unwell unlucky untrue unkind disagree distrust disobey disappear dishonest

2 a unwell b disappear c distrust d unlucky e unfair f disobey g dishonest h untrue i unkind j disagree

3 a unlucky b disobey c disappear d disagree e untrue f unkind g distrust h dishonest i unfair j unwell

Unit 17

1 useful colourful powerful thoughtful helpful useless colourless powerless thoughtless helpless

2 a useless b helpless c powerless d thoughtless e colourless f powerful g helpful h colourful i useful j thoughtful

3 a helpful b colourful c useless d thoughtless e powerful

Unit 18

2

verb	add **ing**	verb	add **ing**
hide	hiding	shut	shutting
drive	driving	run	running
bite	biting	win	winning
ride	riding	wag	wagging
smile	smiling	dig	digging

3 a hiding b running c winning d riding e smiling f digging g driving h wagging i biting j shutting

Unit 19

2 angry cross frightened miserable pleased

3 bored excited lonely shy unhappy

4 a miserable b excited c frightened d bored e pleased f cross g angry h unhappy i lonely j shy

Unit 20

2 bellowed exclaimed grumbled joked murmured

3 demanded howled pleaded shouted whispered

4 a joked b demanded c shouted d bellowed e grumbled f pleaded g howled h whispered i exclaimed j murmured

Spelling test answers

Test 1

1 ______________________
2 ______________________
3 ______________________
4 ______________________
5 ______________________
6 ______________________
7 ______________________
8 ______________________
9 ______________________
10 ______________________

Score ____

Test 2

1 ______________________
2 ______________________
3 ______________________
4 ______________________
5 ______________________
6 ______________________
7 ______________________
8 ______________________
9 ______________________
10 ______________________

Score ____

Test 3

1 ______________________
2 ______________________
3 ______________________
4 ______________________
5 ______________________
6 ______________________
7 ______________________
8 ______________________
9 ______________________
10 ______________________

Score ____

Test 4

1 ______________________
2 ______________________
3 ______________________
4 ______________________
5 ______________________
6 ______________________
7 ______________________
8 ______________________
9 ______________________
10 ______________________

Score ____

Test 5

1 ______
2 ______
3 ______
4 ______
5 ______
6 ______
7 ______
8 ______
9 ______
10 ______

Score ____

Test 6

1 ______
2 ______
3 ______
4 ______
5 ______
6 ______
7 ______
8 ______
9 ______
10 ______

Score ____

Test 7

1 ______
2 ______
3 ______
4 ______
5 ______
6 ______
7 ______
8 ______
9 ______
10 ______

Score ____

Test 8

1 ______
2 ______
3 ______
4 ______
5 ______
6 ______
7 ______
8 ______
9 ______
10 ______

Score ____

Test 9

1 ______________________________
2 ______________________________
3 ______________________________
4 ______________________________
5 ______________________________
6 ______________________________
7 ______________________________
8 ______________________________
9 ______________________________
10 ______________________________

Score ____

Test 10

1 ______________________________
2 ______________________________
3 ______________________________
4 ______________________________
5 ______________________________
6 ______________________________
7 ______________________________
8 ______________________________
9 ______________________________
10 ______________________________

Score ____

Test 11

1 ______________________________
2 ______________________________
3 ______________________________
4 ______________________________
5 ______________________________
6 ______________________________
7 ______________________________
8 ______________________________
9 ______________________________
10 ______________________________

Score ____

Test 12

1 ______________________________
2 ______________________________
3 ______________________________
4 ______________________________
5 ______________________________
6 ______________________________
7 ______________________________
8 ______________________________
9 ______________________________
10 ______________________________

Score ____

Test 13

1 ______________________________
2 ______________________________
3 ______________________________
4 ______________________________
5 ______________________________
6 ______________________________
7 ______________________________
8 ______________________________
9 ______________________________
10 ______________________________

Score ____

Test 14

1 ______________________________
2 ______________________________
3 ______________________________
4 ______________________________
5 ______________________________
6 ______________________________
7 ______________________________
8 ______________________________
9 ______________________________
10 ______________________________

Score ____

Test 15

1 ______________________________
2 ______________________________
3 ______________________________
4 ______________________________
5 ______________________________
6 ______________________________
7 ______________________________
8 ______________________________
9 ______________________________
10 ______________________________

Score ____

Test 16

1 ______________________________
2 ______________________________
3 ______________________________
4 ______________________________
5 ______________________________
6 ______________________________
7 ______________________________
8 ______________________________
9 ______________________________
10 ______________________________

Score ____

Test 17

1 ______________________________
2 ______________________________
3 ______________________________
4 ______________________________
5 ______________________________
6 ______________________________
7 ______________________________
8 ______________________________
9 ______________________________
10 ______________________________

Score ____

Test 18

1 ______________________________
2 ______________________________
3 ______________________________
4 ______________________________
5 ______________________________
6 ______________________________
7 ______________________________
8 ______________________________
9 ______________________________
10 ______________________________

Score ____

Test 19

1 ______________________________
2 ______________________________
3 ______________________________
4 ______________________________
5 ______________________________
6 ______________________________
7 ______________________________
8 ______________________________
9 ______________________________
10 ______________________________

Score ____

Test 20

1 ______________________________
2 ______________________________
3 ______________________________
4 ______________________________
5 ______________________________
6 ______________________________
7 ______________________________
8 ______________________________
9 ______________________________
10 ______________________________

Score ____